Table of Contents

About the Authors

Emily Burrows, Ed.S., is a seventh grade middle school teacher at Arnall Middle School in Newnan, Georgia. Mrs. Burrows is a veteran teacher, having taught in both Georgia and Kentucky. She has collaborated with resource teachers and has taught both students with autism and Asperger's Syndrome. Her research project for the Ed.S. Degree at West Georgia State University (with this booklet as a result) has given her further knowledge on meeting the classroom needs of the students with Asperger's Syndrome.

Sheila Wagner, M.Ed., is an Assistant Director of the Emory Autism Center at Emory University in Atlanta, Georgia. Ms. Wagner is also the MONARCH Program Coordinator and has conducted the EAC School Inclusion Project for 11 years, affecting over 600 students with Autism Spectrum Disorders. Ms. Wagner has published two books on inclusive programming for students with this disorder with a third in progress, and is a national and international lecturer on educating students with autism and Asperger's Syndrome. Information on her two books, *Inclusive Programming for Elementary Students with Autism* (1999), which won the ASA Literary Award for 2000, and *Inclusive Programming for the Middle School Student with Autism and Asperger's Syndrome* can be obtained by contacting Future Horizons, Inc. at www.FutureHorizons-autism.com

Preface

As mandated by federal law (Individuals with Disabilities Education Act-I.D.E.A.), educational programming for students with disabilities must be provided in the least restrictive environment, including the student diagnosed with Asperger's Syndrome. Do we as professional teachers know how to provide this programming within the context of our teaching?

The purpose of this guide is to help educators (teachers and administrators) become acquainted with identifying and meeting the needs of the student with Asperger's Syndrome. Public school, while often difficult for typical students, can be a nightmare for those students with Asperger's Syndrome. Without information and training in this disability, teachers face confusion and frustration in light of the unusual behaviors and lack of social skills. Without training, students with Asperger's Syndrome are misidentified and often blamed for behaviors that are a direct result of their disability. It is hoped that this guide will lead teachers to a better understanding of Asperger's Syndrome and help the students with AS have a richer, more enjoyable educational experience.

What is Asperger's Syndrome?

In the gifted classes, John's academic achievement is strong. He is not a bully; he has no mean attributes at all. For two years he has been selling candy and helping at car washes to raise money for the 8th Grade trip to Washington, D. C. As the date of the trip draws closer, none of the other boys are willing to share a room with him. The outcome: he ends up not going. This scenario is all-too familiar to people who have Asperger's Syndrome (Safran, 2002).

More than 50 years ago, Hans Asperger, a Viennese pediatrician, identified a pattern of behavior that included lack of empathy, inability to form friendships, one-sided conversations, intense absorption in a special interest, and clumsy motor movements. Now known as Asperger's Syndrome, the disability is more and more recognized in today's society.

The most recognized definition of Asperger's Syndrome comes from the Diagnostic and Statistical Manual IV-TR of Mental Disorders (American Psychiatric Association, 2000). A diagnosis of Asperger's requires certain symptoms be present, including at least two indicators of impairment in social interaction, and at least one in the area of restrictive interest and stereotyped behaviors or rituals.

Research confirms that Asperger's Syndrome is a serious social and communication disorder that can result in devastating effects. However, with proper support and training, these students can progress and learn, and go on to lead happy and productive lives to the best of their ability.

FAST FACTS - Asperger's Syndrome:

Examples of social impairment include:

- Poor eye contact.

- Problems interacting with peers.

- Difficulty making/keeping friends.

- May invade personal space.

- Lack of appreciation of social/emotional cues.

- Inappropriate facial affect in relation to situation.

- Difficulties with understanding other people's perspective.

Examples of restrictive interests include:

- Over-focus on particular interests to the point of being "a little professor."

- Difficulty with changes & transitions.

- Repetitive motor movements, i.e. rocking, toe-walking.

- Preoccupation with parts of objects.

- Low frustration tolerance; poor coping skills.

- Insistence on having "their own way."

Examples of difficulties with communication impairment include:

- Difficulties with pragmatic language are inherent, i.e., limited understanding of non-verbal cues, gestures, body language; lack of understanding of sarcasm and jokes; poor vocal tone; preference for talking on their topics only; interruption of others; difficulty processing abstract concepts and work that calls for inferential reasoning.

Other characteristics:

- Evidence of fine/gross motor delays.

- Problems with organizational skills.

- Average to above-average IQ.

- On-time language development.

Asperger's Syndrome is recognized as a separate and distinct category under Pervasive Developmental Disorder and is considered part of the Autistism Spectrum Disorders.

The ability to interact and communicate with others appropriately in a social way is significantly impaired within Asperger's Syndrome. The child with this disorder has an interest in people socially; in fact, he desperately wants friends, but doesn't know how to get them or keep them. Teachers often fail to recognize the uneven skill development of students with Asperger's Syndrome because the students give the impression that they know more than they actually do. The deficits of students with

Asperger's Syndrome are hidden by their advanced vocabulary and parrot-like responses. Some students may be compliant and unassertive.

In examining the uneven skill development, teachers often become enamored with the high academic potential and forget about the "iceberg" of delayed skills underlying the IQ level. When this happens, teacher expectations are set impossibly high for the student. Consequently, the student experiences frustration, anger, and he or she may melt down because he or she does not know how to solve the problem. At this point, you may witness the student shutting down, refusing to do school work, exhibiting depression and sometimes, dropping out of school.

The behaviors that the student with AS subsequently exhibits can set the stage for punishment-based consequences, poor academic performance, notoriety amongst peers and becoming a target for the bullies in school.

So where do we start?

Teaching Strategies for the Student with Asperger's Syndrome

All school personnel will need to learn about the characteristics of Asperger's Syndrome and specific teaching strategies that are proven to be effective for students with this disability in the classroom. The intelligence and vocabulary traits that these students display often hinder recognition of the underlying disability with the result that many do not receive the support or assistance from special education or resource classrooms. For this reason, it is imperative that teachers become well-acquainted with methods that can be used to refer for services, or to support the student with Asperger's Syndrome in the regular education classes.

Students with Asperger's Syndrome have very specific talents. They tend to excel when given visual supports for assignments and positive recognition for their accomplishments. They may experience difficulty with abstractions in text and misinterpret the meaning of the passage.

Problems a student with AS may experience in the academic environment can be many, including distraction or inattention; tunnel vision; high rote memory ability, but poor abstract reasoning; visual versus auditory processing; poor problem solving ability; lack of motor skills coordination; and inconsistent motivation for work.

We will look at each of these areas in depth and offer solutions:

Impairment in social interaction is an issue educators must address when instructing a child with Asperger's Syndrome. They tend to talk "to" people or lecture them, rather than talk "with" them in a reciprocal social manner. These students often take everything they hear literally, thereby misinterpreting intent of text and statements and others' perspectives. Educators can incorporate the following strategies to improve social skills:

- Educate peers on all disabilities, including Asperger's, but do not pinpoint this student out as having AS.

- Students with AS can be peer tutors to other students as well as the one being tutored. Use both strategies whenever possible.

- Capitalize teachable moments and imbed social skills into all lessons.

- Conduct routine social skills assessments to view areas of need, twice a year is recommended for pre- post assessment.

- Develop formal or informal buddy systems for all students, so the student will not be blatantly identified.

- Teach the student "how" to function in a team so he will do better in group situations.

- Implement direct and incidental instruction in social skills (i.e., social stories, problem analysis, role playing).

- Conduct weekly or bi-weekly social skills training (can be conducted by special, or regular teacher, counselor, teacher mentor, etc.).

- Coordinate all teachers in knowing the weekly skills addressed.

- Use prompting and reinforcement.

- Establish routines and structures to practice using appropriate social skills throughout day.

- Have set routines established that will allow the student to perform the skill and receive feed-back.

- Teach appropriate social interaction with peers, through supervised, small groups at lunch, before or after school, etc., where typical students practice the targeted lessons and act as role models. In middle and high school, choose more mature students to participate. Feedback can be given to the entire group, or to the student individually (not in front of the others).

FAST FACTS - Behavioral Strategies:

Educators must also address the issue of restricted range of interests and inappropriate behaviors. Children with Asperger's Syndrome often have peculiar interests and sometimes, outbursts. They may become fixated on one topic wishing to spend all of their time talking on that topic.

Those with Asperger's may have very low frustration tolerance and coping skills. Educators can incorporate the following strategies to improve behavioral skills:

- Limit time spent on preservative interest or pair it after other activities.

- Use positive reinforcement to shape and teach replacement behaviors.

- Allow a limited number of questions to be asked about a particular topic.

- Set firm expectations and be consistent. Teach strategies to calm down.

- Use their intense interests to introduce new ideas or to teach subject material.

- Structure free time.

- If student is upset, limit verbal cues to specific, short and concrete cues. Do not attempt to engage in conversation with the student until he or she is calm. Limit eye contact when the student is upset.

One of the impairments that educators need to consider when teaching students with Asperger's Syndrome, is sensitivity to change. Problems with transitions and changes can lead to any level of inappropriate behaviors. Children with the disorder tend to perform tasks better when presented in a consistent or predictable manner, but can learn flexibility when taught systematically and in a positive manner.

In order to best meet this need and reduce problem behaviors, educators can incorporate the following strategies into the daily routine:

- Provide a predictable environment.

- Use positive behavior management and feedback with a strongly preferred motivator, offered at the end or for task completion.

- Avoid calling attention to the students mistakes in front of peers.

- Minimize transitions in the day.

- Avoid surprises (prepare student in advance for change in schedule, i.e., field trip, pep rally, assembly).

- Tie performance of transitions to a positive behavior plan.

- Carefully structure seating arrangements.

- Do not seat the student with Asperger's Syndrome next to an aggressive student or known bully.

- Seat the student by a "peer buddy" who could serve as a social or behavioral translator.

- Avoid self-selection of groups.

- Seat the student near to where the teacher usually lectures.

FAST FACTS - Communication Impairment:

Although language milestones came in on time when the child was little, and students with AS are highly verbal, there is tremendous difficulty with language and using it during routine classwork and in interacting with others. Difficulties with pragmatic language skills are inherent with this disability. Here are some areas of difficulty when focusing on supports for the student:

- Overly dramatic gestural use.

- Pedantic (overly formal) speech.

- Provides too much detail when talking on topics of interest.

- Absent or reduced eye contact when speaking.

- Understanding jokes & sarcasm.

- Reading non-verbal body language of others, including vocal tone, inflection, etc.

- Understanding idioms.

- Isn't a "flexible" speaker; usually is an overly concrete, literal thinker.

- Understanding others' perspectives (usually see only their own viewpoint).

- Making inferences on situations.

- Understanding and expressing emotions adequately.

Teaching strategies to improve communication skills include:

- Pragmatic language therapy.

- Role-playing with peers.

- Self-analysis through videotaping.

- Self-rating of performance.

- Explanations and examples of appropriate skill use.

- Setting up examples to problem-solve.

- Teaching emotions through facial recognition programs.

- Explaining why situations go wrong with peers.

FAST FACTS - Sensory Impairment:

Students with Asperger's Syndrome often face high sensitivities to noise levels, smells, textures, tags in clothing, lines in socks, etc. This means that you may see high resistance or problem behaviors when going into the gymnasium, cafeteria, or chaotic environment. The student may call out to other students to be quiet, try to isolate themselves from groups, repeatedly take off shoes or socks, or become upset when teachers limit access to something that he or she wants to hold or feel.

In order to best help the student with this area, consider:

- Assessing environment for chaos, relevant objects or activities that the student is sensitive to. Change, eliminate or diminish whenever possible.

- Desensitization programs (gradual introduction) to the area of sensitivity with strong reinforcers attached.

- Offering times or areas to "get away from the noise and calm down" when they can't handle it.

- Self-regulation programs so the student can understand their own needs and how to manage them.

FAST FACTS - Instructional Strategies:

Students with Asperger's Syndrome have endless potential when teachers recognize their needs and structure the environment for success (Myles, 1998). This can be done through use of visual cues, graphic organizers, outlines, verbal cues, and providing help in problem solving.

• Visual Cues

Students with Asperger's Syndrome receive the most benefit from instruction when material is presented visually rather than auditorily. Students may need visual schedules typed and hung in their lockers, placed in notebooks, agendas, or on their desks.

• Graphic Organizers

Graphic organizers provide a concrete framework from which to understand abstract concepts. Students use key terms and words to show relationships; this is particularly useful with content material. The organizers often enhance the learning of students with Asperger's Syndrome because they allow more thought processing time and add the visual component. Types of graphic organizers are:

- Hierarchical

- Conceptual

- Sequential

- Cyclical

- Venn Diagram

- Overlapping Concepts

- Cause & Effect

- Plot Diagram

• Outlines

Many times the student with Asperger's Syndrome is not proficient at taking notes—an outline could list main points and details. If the teacher provides the student with this tool ahead of time, he is free to listen. Copies of lesson plans can be very helpful.

• Verbal Cues

Concrete verbal cues such as "this is a main point," assist the student in knowing what is important and what is not.

• Problem Solving

Many students with Asperger's Syndrome are capable of engaging in high-level thinking, but they may select one problem solving strategy and use it, regardless of the situation. For example, if his locker does not open, he may keep trying the combination. He may try it five to six times unsuccessfully. This may result in confusion, frustration and a loss of coping strategies.

Students with Asperger's Syndrome frequently have difficulty with word problems, estimation, algebra, and geometry, all of which require high-level thinking and abstraction. They may have difficulty understanding another person's perspective when asked to project opinions.

Many times the student with Asperger's Syndrome who has demonstrated average or high cognitive ability will still have difficulty with the regular core curriculum. It is often necessary for the regular education teacher to make adaptations to the curriculum to allow for success.

Ways to identify and modify materials and activities include:

- Size - abbreviate assignments.

- Time - give extra time to complete assignments.

- Level of support - give extra help, if needed.

- Input - type notes for the student or allow him to take your or a peer's notes home.

- Output - allow student to respond verbally instead of writing responses; can use a computer instead.

- Difficulty - increase or decrease level of difficulty (may use calculator).

- Participation - limit the amount required (Wagner, 2002), or explain expectations for participation clearly and connect it to the positive behavior plan.

- Teaching format - vary teaching formats during class periods by providing lecture/demonstration, hands-on experiences, experiential learning, cooperative learning, projects, research, and one-to-one learning.

- Instructional grouping - whole group, small group, peer buddies, and individual grouping.

- Rate of instruction - stop periodically to assess comprehension and give small breaks.

- Setting - change the setting of instruction (library, outside, computer lab).

Many times the teacher's style of delivery may not be clear enough for the student with Asperger's Syndrome to understand, making it difficult for the student to comply with cues or directions. Sometimes the cues delivered by the parent for doing homework may vary or contradict the teacher's (Wagner, 2002). Close coordination between home and school will be needed throughout. Parents should report back to teachers how much time is spent on homework, so that adjustments in assignments can be made.

Educators need to be prepared to overcome the issue of poor concentration. Students with Asperger's Syndrome often require frequent redirection and may be easily distracted, as these children can have a short attention span. To compensate for this inability to concentrate, educators can implement the following modifications into their classroom:

- Motivate them to increase time on tasks through concrete reinforcement.

- Teach in cooperative or paired learning groups.

- Modify academics, depending on the student's IEP, including reduced homework load, switching to computer generated output, or abbreviated assignments.

- Students with Asperger's like to "fit in" and be like everyone else. If a paraprofessional is assigned, she needs to become "invisible" and not be glued to the student, but circulate the room to help others.

- Seat the student with Asperger's Syndrome near the front of the room so teacher can deliver non-verbal and verbal cues quietly.

FAST FACTS - Other Strategies:

Educators must address the issue of poor fine and gross motor coordination, as well. Many students with Asperger's Syndrome may appear awkward and clumsy and are unsuccessful in activities requiring use of motor skills. Fine motor skills involving penmanship may mean laborious writing and poor handwriting. Gross motor problems can mean lack of coordination for team sports, clumsy and awkward running or walking gait, and the excuse for peers to tease them. In addition, organizational skills are usually poorly developed. Educators can help the student overcome these problems by incorporating the following modifications into their classroom.

Modifications for Fine Motor Skills:

- Eliminate repetitive writing assignments.

- Have peer take notes for student.

- When assigning timed units of work, allot extra time for completion of work. Allow use of computer whenever possible, (or tape recorder for taking notes).

- Teach keyboarding skills early.

- Provide laptop or word processor for older grades.

Modifications for Gross Motor Skills:

- Avoid pushing a student with Asperger's Syndrome to be competitive.

- Consider adaptive P.E. evaluation to improve muscle tone.

- Offer alternatives to "dressing out" in the locker room.

- Monitor activities that require hand/arm-eye coordination.

Modifications for Organizational Skills:

- Color-coded dividers in the student's notebook.

- Break assignments down into smaller components and set a specific deadline for each one.

- An AM/PM notebook (depending on the student).

- A "to do" list (either agenda size or larger).

- Using graphic organizers (KWL Chart, Story Organizers, Project Planning).

- Have resource teacher check list of assignments for accuracy at end of day.

- Have student email assignment form to himself at end of school, so he, or his parent, can open it on his computer at home that night.

- Have student email finished assignments back to the teacher if possible.

FAST FACTS - Problem Solving:

If, after careful analysis and making use of the strategies listed in this pamphlet, you are still facing difficulties in teaching this student, where do you go from here? To solve the problems, ask yourself the following questions:

1. Are my instructions clear?

2. Are my sentences short?

3. Am I avoiding using sarcasm or idioms?

4. Am I consistent with the other teachers on my team who also teach this student?

5. Am I using visual supplemental materials?

6. Do I allow enough time for processing?

7. Am I asking too much information from this student?

8. Are my expectations too high or too low?

9. Have we been taking enough data?

10. Is the behavior plan effective?

11. Are we using strong motivators?

12. Does my student have friends?

13. Is the student being teased/bullied?

14. Is the student having the same problems at home?

If you still have difficulties and cannot answer some of these questions, then call a team meeting to discuss and conduct a more formal analysis.

FAST FACTS - Bullying of Asperger's Syndrome Students:

In order to actively participate in the prevention of bullying of the student with Asperger's Syndrome, we as educators and school systems need to:

- Understand the disorder of Asperger's Syndrome.

- Monitor and supervise unstructured time consistently and carefully.

- Educate all the peers on bullying.

- Teach social skills (through direct & indirect instruction).

- Have students mediate solutions

- Intervene early (Olweus, 1993).

Teasing and bullying contribute greatly to the levels of depression and thoughts of suicide that we see in the population of Asperger's Syndrome. Many drop out of school entirely at this age, due to this occurrence. All teachers and school staff need to understand that bullying can occur on a very sophisticated level with the typical peers ensuring that the teachers do not see it happen. Therefore, it is imperative that all school staff recognize that bullying can occur in the best of schools and work to prevent it from happening through a pro-active approach.

Because of their poor social skills and their awkward, gross motor skills, students with Asperger's Syndrome are perfect victims for bullying. They have a tremendous social inability and can be teased by other students because of their awkward and immature demeanor. Students with Asperger's Syndrome are extremely bright in some areas, yet very socially immature. Because they do not make friends, they can suffer from high levels of depression and poor self-image. They often really desire friends, but they do not know how to make or keep them.

As teachers, we need to monitor what goes on inside the classroom, as well as outside it. Research states the majority of bullying occurs at school, rather than on the way to school (Olweus, 1993). We are responsible for providing a safe environment. Therefore, we need to support students with Asperger's Syndrome by:

- Accepting that bullying occurs; especially in schools.

- Making certain they have at least one supportive friend or teacher to turn to.

- Teaching skills that can deflect bullying.

- Having real consequences for the bullies.

- Seating the student with Asperger's Syndrome away from students who might tend to bully.

- Providing supervision in areas of risk.

Schools can create an atmosphere where healthy choice-making is encouraged. Rules, rights, responsibilities, and respect must be enforced. All students have the right to learn in a safe, non-threatening environment. Students must respect the rights of classmates, as well as their own.

Through prevention of bullying in the school environment, the student with Asperger's Syndrome will feel safe and accepted. A positive classroom environment will help all students to work together, promote self-esteem, and treat others with kindness and mutual respect.

FAST FACTS - Wrapping It Up: A Final Word From the Authors!

Students who have Asperger's Syndrome are truly wonderful, enchanting and a gift to teachers. They can learn, progress and be strong contributors to our society and it is hoped that you will thoroughly enjoy these students, learn from them, and assist their learning throughout the educational years.

We hope that you will take the time to learn more about this disorder and about your student in particular. It is an experience you will not want to miss, as the lessons that are learned from this individual will provide you with an insight and a personal analysis of your own teaching talents.

This FAST FACTS pamphlet outlines only a few of the issues and strategies; it is hoped that you will further investigate this disorder and share the information with other teachers, administrators, or parents. We promise you will be a far better teacher for knowing this student!

References:

American Psych Association. *Diagnostic & Statistical Manual of Mental Disorders* (Washington, DC: American Psychiatric Association Press, 2000).

Attwood, T., *Asperger's Syndrome: A guide for Parents and Professionals* (London and Philadelphia: Jessica Kingsley Publishers, 1998).

Autism Society of America, *Shaping Our Future* [Brochure] (Bethesda, MD).

Beane, A.L., *The Bully-Free Classroom* (Minneapolis, MN: Free Spirit Publishing Company, 1999).

[Emory Austin Center] *Characteristics of Autism and Asperger's Syndrome* (Atlanta, GA.).

Fine, L., *Educational Implications for the Middle School Asperger's Syndrome Student* (Carrollton, GA., 2002).

Myles, B. & Simpson, R., *Asperger's Syndrome: A Guide for Educators and Parents* (Austin, TX: Pro-ed Publishing Company, 1998).

Safran, J., *Supporting Students with Asperger's Syndrome in General Education*, *Teaching Exceptional Children*, 34, (5).

Wagner, S., *Bullies, Thugs and Little Monsters: Prevention, Training and Supporting Students with Autism/Asperger's Syndrome* (Power Point Presentation, 2003).

Other Suggested Resources:

Cumine, V., Leach, J., & Stevenson, G., *Asperger's Syndrome: A Practical Guide for Teachers* (London: David Fulton Publishers, 1998).

Gray, Carol, *Comic Strip Conversations* (Arlington, TX: Future Horizons, Inc., 1994).

Gray, Carol. *The New Social Storybook* (Arlington, TX: Future Horizons, Inc., 1994).

Moyers, Rebecca, *Addressing the Challenging Behavior of Children with High-Functioning Autism/Asperger's Syndrome in the Classroom: A Guide for Teachers and Parents* (London /Philadelphia. Jessica Kingsley Publishers, 2002).

Myles, Brenda, *Asperger's Syndrome: A Guide for Educators & Parents* (Austin, TX: Pro-ed, 1998).

Myles, B. and Adreon, D., *Asperger's Syndrome & Adolescence: Practical Solutions* (Shawnee Mission, KS: Autism/Asperger Publishing Co, 2001).

Olweus, D., *Bullying at School* (Blackwell Publ, 1993).

Romanowski, P. and Kirby, B., *The Oasis Guide to Asperger's Syndrome* (New York: Crown Publishing Company, 2001).

Wagner, S., *Build Me a Bridge, Autism-Asperger's Digest*, 10-13.

Wagner, S., *Inclusive Programming for the Elementary School Student with Autism* (Arlington, TX.: Future Horizons, Inc., 1999).